D1393827

NEWMAN'S UNIVERSITY CHURCH

Newman's University Church

a history and guide

J. Anthony Gaughan

BIBL. COLLEGA
S.S. CORDIS
S.J. LIMERICK

KINGDOM BOOKS

Printed in the Republic of Ireland
at the Leinster Leader, Naas, County Kildare,
for
KINGDOM BOOKS
56 Newtownpark Avenue, Blackrock, County Dublin

First published 1997

BRITISH LIBRARY CATALOGUING IN PUBLICATION DATA

Gaughan, J. Anthony (John Anthony), 1932-
    Newman's University Church: a history and guide
    1. Newman, John Henry, 1801-1890 2. University Church –
    History 3. Church buildings – Great Britain – Guidebooks
    4. Cardinals – Great Britain – Biography
    I Title
    726.5'0941
            ISBN 0 9524567 0 2

Copyright under the Berne Convention, all rights reserved. Apart from fair deal-
ing for study or review, no part of this publication may be reproduced, stored in
a retrieval system or transmitted, in any form or by any means, electronic,
mechanical, photocopying, recording, or otherwise, without the prior permission
of Kingdom Books.

© J. Anthony Gaughan 1997

CONTENTS

LIST OF ILLUSTRATIONS

FOREWORD

As president of University College Dublin I compliment Father J. Anthony Gaughan on his research work which has produced this most interesting account of the history and features of Newman's University Church. University College Dublin received its charter in 1908 but traces its origins to the Catholic University of Ireland with John Henry Newman as its first rector. The historic association continues to this day with University College Dublin continuing to have full access to the church. Although most faculties of the College are now located on the Belfield campus, University Church is well known and loved by students and graduates; it is a favoured venue for marriage ceremonies and religious celebrations of class re-unions. It is good to know that the association will continue into the twenty-first century.

ART COSGROVE
President
University College Dublin
1 January 1997

To

SEÁN COMERFORD
dedicated and kindly sacristan
of Newman's University Church

PREFATORY NOTE

This guide presents a sketch of the circumstances in which University Church was built and the objects which its founder, John Henry Newman, had in mind for it.

The detailed description of the artistic features and decoration is intended to be of use to the discerning visitor who wishes to appreciate the good taste of Newman and the artistic genius of John Hungerford Pollen, the church's architect, decorator and painter. Further information can be acquired from the perceptive treatment of the subject in C. P. Curran's *Newman House and University Church* (Dublin, n.d.), Eileen Kane's 'John Henry Newman's Catholic University Church in Dublin', *Studies,* summer/autumn 1977 and Louis McRedmond's *Thrown among strangers: John Henry Newman in Ireland* (Dublin 1990).

In connection with the preparation of this booklet, I wish to thank: Art Cosgrove for providing the Foreword, Sister Madeleine Kisner, A.S.C., for her *haiku* on Newman, printed as Appendix 1, Fr Liam Rigney for allowing me to consult and use his unpublished doctoral thesis and all those who gave me information, especially those whose names appear on p. 54.

I am indebted to Mrs Eileen Francis, Eileen Kane, Helen Murray, Fr Ernan Neville, Maurice O'Connell, Peter O'Keeffe, Pat O'Kelly, Susan Waine and Fr Gregory Winterton of the Birmingham Oratory for their encouragement and help.

My special thanks are due to Seán Comerford who has served in University Church since 1947 and whose attachment to, and knowledge of, the church is truly unique.

I am grateful to Jarlath Hayes for the design and layout of the booklet and to Stan Hickey for preparing it for printing.

This guide is offered as a token of my appreciation of having had the privilege of ministering in University Church from 1983 to 1988.

J. ANTHONY GAUGHAN
56 Newtownpark Avenue
Blackrock
Co Dublin
1 January 1997

PART 1

HISTORY

During the nineteenth century Irish Catholics intensified their agitation to secure their right to Catholic education for their children. They considered this to be a just demand as Protestant children had access to Protestant education. By the middle of the century they had focussed on securing a complete system of Catholic education which included a Catholic university. There was only one university, the University of Dublin, with its single college, Trinity College. It had been founded by Queen Elizabeth I (1533-1603) by charter of incorporation, dated 3 March 1592. It was essentially a Protestant university in its character and Catholics had been effectively excluded from it by the 'Laudian statutes' of King Charles I (1600-49) in 1637 which made the Anglican faith and practice obligatory for its students. The Catholic Relief Act of 1793 and the Royal Letter of 1794 attempted to remedy this effective exclusion of Catholics by a partial concession which enabled them to enter the college and obtain degrees, but not tutorships, fellowships or foundation-scholarships. Nonetheless, Catholics continued to be unwilling to enter a university where they were regarded as second-class citizens and where none of their fellow-religionists could hold a teaching position.

Struggle for Catholic Education

Various proposals were put forward to remedy this situation and finally in 1845 a bill was introduced in the House of Commons for the establishment of the Queen's Colleges. The three colleges were to be situated in Belfast, Cork and either Limerick or Galway, and to be united as constituent colleges of a new university. These new colleges were to be non-denominational and State-endowed. There were to be no religious tests on entrance or on taking a degree, no religious instruction except what might be privately provided by the various religious bodies, and no religious considerations were to count in the appointment or dismissal of officials.

Queen's Colleges

Irish Catholics were suspicious of this imposition on them of a system which the English people themselves had to a large extent repudiated. Oxford and Cambridge were strictly denominational. Trinity College, Dublin, was and continued to be denominational by virtue of its charter. Irish Catholics were divided in their attitude to the proposed colleges. The issue was referred to Rome and rescripts in 1847, 1848 and 1850 condemned the colleges as

Non-Denominational Education

1. John Henry Newman,
c. 1856

2. Paul Cardinal
Cullen,
archbishop of Dublin,
1852-78

unsuitable. The Irish bishops were urged by the Holy See to establish a Catholic university on the model of that recently founded by the Belgian bishops at Louvain.

Meanwhile the government had proceeded with the erection of the Queen's Colleges, which were established in 1845 and opened in 1849 in Belfast, Cork and Galway, the claims of Limerick having been rejected. On 3 September 1850 Queen's University was set up by the government. Based in Dublin Castle, by charter it formally incorporated the three colleges as constituent colleges of a non-denominational university which was to act as their examining and degree-awarding body. The staffing of the colleges gave little encouragement to those Catholics who supported their establishment. Out of sixty professors only seven were Catholics.

In 1850 a national synod of the Catholic bishops was convened at Thurles. It was presided over by the apostolic delegate, Paul Cullen (1803-78), formerly rector of the Irish College, Rome, and then archbishop of Armagh. The synod decided to establish a Catholic university. In 1847 Cullen had made the acquaintance of John Henry Newman (1801-90) when the latter was studying for the priesthood in Rome and in 1851 he invited him to Dublin to lecture on the vexed question of mixed or non-denominational education. He also made Newman a tentative offer of the rectorship of the proposed university. **A Catholic University**

Newman was an imaginative choice. He had been the most prominent member of the Oxford Movement in England. The Movement called for a renewal of the Anglican Church as a more purely religious body. Members were known as the Tractarians from the *Tracts for the times* in which they published their ideas. Newman was vicar of St Mary's University Church, Oxford, and the most prolific of the Tractarians. By his preaching and writing in tracing the origins and outlining the development of the Christian Church he had aroused considerable controversy which reached a climax with the publication of *Tract 90* in 1841. In this, his last *Tract*, he made a systematic effort to reconcile the 39 Articles of statutory Anglican belief with Catholic doctrine. The Anglican authorities exploded with disapproval and in 1843 he retired from Oxford to a private retreat at nearby Littlemore. The worst fears of those who opposed Newman's 'Romanist tendencies' were confirmed when in 1845 he converted to Catholicism. He went to Rome where, in June 1847, he was ordained and joined the Oratorians, whose institute had been founded by St Philip Neri (1515-95). In 1848 he returned to England and established the Oratory at Maryvale, Birmingham. **John Henry Newman**

Newman accepted Cullen's dual invitation. He dreamed of making the proposed university in Dublin a centre of learning and religion for the English-speaking world. On 1 October 1851 he travelled to Ireland and had a preliminary discussion in Thurles with members of a committee charged with setting up the university and on 12 November he was appointed its rector. In May 1852 he delivered the first four of his 'Discourses on the scope and nature of university education' in the Rotunda in Dublin. Owing to the onset of the Achilli trial the remaining five were printed but never delivered. The nine discourses form Part I of *The idea of a university defined and illustrated*, long since regarded as an educational classic. In his discourses Newman did not disappoint Cullen, stressing, as he did, the disadvantages which could arise from mixed or non-denominational education and the Catholic view of what education should be. Due to a lack of unanimity among the trustees of the university there was a delay in calling over Newman to make a start. Eventually on 4 June 1854 he was installed as rector of the new university after High Mass in Dublin's Pro-Cathedral. And on 3 November the university was formally opened at 86 St Stephen's Green.

Newman made ample provision for the spiritual welfare of the students. There were formal courses in religion and other arrangements for their moral welfare. From the outset he planned the erection of a university church which would 'maintain and symbolise that great principle in which we glory as our characteristic, the union of science and religion'. In a note of his plans for the establishment of the Catholic University he wrote:

> The first expedient which suggested itself to me was the erection, or the provision, of a university church. I suppose I had it in mind as early as, or earlier than, any other work.
>
> I thought – (1) Nothing was a more simple and complete advertisement than a large church open for worship; the cheapest advertisement, since, if self-supporting, it cost the university nothing, yet was perpetual and in the light of day. (2) It symbolised the great principle of the university, the indissoluble union of philosophy and religion. (3) It provided for university formal acts, for degree-giving, for solemn lectures and addresses, such as those usual at the opening and closing of the academical year, for the weekly display of the university authorities, etc., a large hall at once, and one which was ennobled by the religious symbols which were its furniture. It interested the clergy in the university, the preachers being taken from all parts of the country.

Finding a suitable site for the university church was not easy. After searching about Newman eventually settled on the garden rear of 87 St Stephen's Green. He considered himself to be very fortunate in being able to acquire it, seeing that it was next door to the main university premises.

Newman was also fortunate in having John Hungerford Pollen (1820-1902) to help him with the building and decoration of the church. Twenty years younger than Newman, he had gone to Oxford in 1838, when Newman's influence was at its height and had heard him preach. In 1846 Pollen was ordained as an Anglican priest and from 1847 onwards ministered at St Saviour's, Leeds. In 1852 he converted to Catholicism. At Oxford Pollen had given evidence of considerable artistic talent. He designed and painted the decoration of Oxford's church of St Peter-le-Bailey. Subsequently he designed and painted the roof of Merton College Chapel. Pollen led a very full life. He built a church in Rhyl, North Wales, and was at various times a fellow of Merton College, private secretary to the Marquis of Ripon, when he was governor general of India, and keeper of the South Kensington (now Victoria and Albert) Museum. At the end of 1854 Pollen, at Newman's invitation, became the honorary professor of fine arts in the new university.

While Pollen was the architect, painter and decorator of University Church, for which he received a salary, the plan and

**John
Hungerford
Pollen**

15

basic ideas with regard to its building and decoration were Newman's. These arose from his enthusiasm for the ancient basilicas of Italy. Pollen recalled that 'he felt a strong attachment to those ancient churches with rude exteriors but solemn and impressive within, recalling the early history of the Church, as it gradually felt its way in the converted empire ...' Thus Newman disclosed to Pollen what he had in mind for his church: 'My idea was to build a large barn and decorate it in the style of a basilica, with Irish marbles and copies of standard pictures.' The church was to be large, as Newman envisaged it being used as a lecture theatre and graduation hall as well as a place of worship. It is interesting to note that barn-churches were typical in Ireland of the late eighteenth and early nineteenth centuries. They were usually built of rubble-stone rendered, with a roof of moderate pitch and were often T-shaped.

Work was begun on the church in May 1855 and it was opened a year later on Ascension Day with 'Our Lady, Seat of Wisdom' as its titular. The interior decoration was not finished for the formal opening but it went ahead rapidly and was completed by the end of the summer.

Newman's Resignation The year 1856-57 was the last of Newman's residence in Dublin. All along he had continued as superior of the Oratory in Birmingham. Thus less than half his time was spent in Ireland. In spite of this unsatisfactory state of affairs, the university made steady, if slow, progress. By then, however, the four Catholic archbishops, who were the principal trustees of the Catholic University, were becoming disenchanted with regard to the university in general and Newman's involvement in it in particular.

The leaders of the Irish Church, whose adherents were just about recovering from the ravages of the Famine, were finding it increasingly difficult to justify expenditure on it. Besides, some of the archbishops were not impressed by Newman's busying himself with other projects in England for more than half of each year. And a further reason for dissatisfaction was Newman's native incapacity for practical organisation.

Moreover, his tendency to select English professors and officials to staff the university indicated a lack of sensitivity to Irish national aspirations. There were, however, some notable exceptions in this regard. Apart from securing Eugene O'Curry (1796-1862) to serve as professor of archaeology and Irish history, Newman appointed John O'Hagan (1822-90) ('Slieve Gullion' and 'Caroline Wilhelmina Amelia' of *The Nation*, organ of Young Ireland) to the chair of political economy and Denis Florence McCarthy (1817-82) ('Desmond' of *The Nation*) to that of English literature. Of O'Hagan and McCarthy Newman wrote: 'There were a knot of

4. Fr William Henry Anderdon, S.J., c. 1880

men who in 1848 had been quasi-rebels. They were clever men and had cooled down, most of them. Dr David Moriarty [1814-77] [president, All Hallows College and later bishop of Kerry] introduced them to me and I made them professors. They are the ablest men who belonged to the university ...'

Newman was aware of the disenchantment of the trustees and, in spite of attempts by the professors and some clerical friends to dissuade him, submitted his resignation to the archbishops in November 1858. It was not formally accepted until August 1859 and he remained rector until that date, but ceased to exercise any function.

Among the clerical friends Newman left behind was Fr William H. Anderdon (1816-90). He also had formerly been an Anglican priest and he had served in St Margaret's parish, Leicester, from 1846 to 1850. A nephew of the archbishop of Westminster, Henry Edward Manning (1808-92) and an accomplished preacher, Newman had appointed him chaplain to University Church, a post he held from 1856 to 1863. He joined the Jesuits in 1872 and spent most of the rest of his life preaching missions and retreats in the Greater Manchester area.

William H. Anderdon

5. *Rev Dr Bartholomew Woodlock, rector of the Catholic University of Ireland, 1861-79*

6. *Mgr Henry Neville (1820-89): He was ordained for the diocese of Cork in 1847 at St Patrick's College, Maynooth, where he was appointed professor of philosophy in 1850 and succeeded to a chair in theology in 1852. After resigning on grounds of ill-health in 1867 he ministered in Cork diocese becoming parish priest of St Finbarr's, dean and vicar-general in 1875. He retained these diocesan offices, while acting as rector of the Catholic University of Ireland from 1879 to 1883.*

In 1861 Newman was succeeded by Dr Bartholomew Woodlock (1819-1902). Before his involvement with the new university, Woodlock, a priest of the archdiocese of Dublin, was well-known as an educationalist and as a social activist. He was associated with Fr John Hand from the outset in the establishment of the Missionary College of All Hallows, whose object was the education of priests for the foreign and colonial English-speaking missions. A key-member of the staff from 1842 to 1861 as professor of dogmatic theology, Italian and sacred ceremonies, he was president from 1854 to 1861. His many active interests included his being a founder member of the Society of St Vincent de Paul in Ireland in 1844, and spiritual director of the Society's Council of Ireland until 1879. He served as bishop of Ardagh and Clonmacnois from 1879 to 1895, when he retired owing to ill-health. As rector of the Catholic University he brought new life into the university. But this did not continue and the university maintained a struggling existence for twenty years, sustained by the hope that the government might be moved to come to its assistance or propose some acceptable alternative. What the university required most of all from the government was never delivered. Its statutes did not receive government recognition and so its degrees, apart from those of the Medical School, had no official public recognition.

Bartholomew Woodlock

The University Education (Ireland) Act of 1879 provided for the dissolution of Queen's University and its replacement by a new, examining university. This was welcomed by most Irish Catholics as merely a first instalment of their right to equal access to university education, hence their struggle to that end continued until the establishment of the National University of Ireland in 1908. After the foundation of the new university, known as the Royal University of Ireland, as an examining body in 1879, the Irish hierarchy met on 3 October 1882 in Holy Cross College, Clonliffe, and decided that thenceforth the Catholic University would consist not of one college but of several, namely: St Patrick's College, Maynooth; University College, St Stephen's Green, Dublin; Holy Cross College, Clonliffe, Dublin; the French College, Blackrock; St Patrick's College, Carlow; St Kieran's College, Kilkenny; St Ignatius' College, Temple Street, Dublin; Mount Carmel College, Terenure, Dublin; and the Medical School, Cecilia Street, Dublin. These colleges were to present their students for the examinations of the Royal University for degrees in arts, medicine, engineering and law. In 1882-83 Monsignor Henry Neville (1820-89), who had succeeded Woodlock in 1879, remained in charge of the Catholic University as a whole but Rev Dr John Egan (1839-91) was president of University College.

University College

In October 1883 University College was entrusted to the Jesuit order and Fr William Delany (1835-1924), an outstanding educationalist, became its president. At that time also the medical school at Cecilia Street was, in effect, separated from the arts and science faculties and was not reincorporated as the university's faculty of medicine until 1908. The entrusting of University College to the Jesuit Fathers was regarded as marking the end of the Catholic University as a living educational institution. It continued to have a nominal existence, as an aggregation of constituent colleges bound together by a rectorial council under the supreme governing body of the Catholic bishops, but had very little practical effect on its constituent colleges. Not least because of the dedication of distinguished members of the Irish province of the Society of Jesus and other sons of St Ignatius Loyola, such as Fr Gerard Manley Hopkins (1844-89), University College and its arts faculty in particular functioned with considerable success for a quarter of a century. Among its *alumni* was James Joyce (1882-1941).

University College, Dublin

In 1908 on the establishment of the National University of Ireland, University College as such ceased to exist, though a certain measure of continuity was preserved between it and the Dublin constituent college of the new university. All its graduates were accepted as members of the body corporate of that university, and the majority of its professors continued in office. The Catholic University as reconstituted in 1882, though it had ceased to function, was not juridically dissolved until 1988 when the trustees donated Newman House, 85 and 86 St Stephen's Green, to University College, Dublin, and sold the two nearby houses, wherein resided the Catholic chaplains of University College, Dublin. Following the completion of this transaction the Irish Catholic bishops erected the St Stephen's chaplaincy at Belfield in 1989.

Cost of University Church

Even after his resignation as rector of the Catholic University in 1859 Newman continued to have concerns with regard to his expenditure on the University Church. To avoid any delay in providing a church for the Catholic University he had decided to pay for its construction and later, hopefully, recoup his expenditure from the trustees of the university. The cost of building the church was £5,600 which was nearly double Newman's original estimate. Donations amounting to £640, including £100 from himself, reduced the debt to £4,960. He was disappointed in his expectation of securing a loan from university funds at low interest. Thus he was forced to pay some £3,000 out of the surplus of the money subscribed for his defence in the Achilli trial and to borrow £2,000 from the Oratory, Birmingham.

20

7. *Fr William Delany, S.J., president of University College, 1883-88, 1897-1909*

8. *Fr Gerard Manley Hopkins, S.J., professor of Greek in University College, 1884-89*

9. *James Augustine Aloysius Joyce, student of University College, 1899-1902*

10. Group of staff and students of University College, c. 1901. Louis McRedmond described the group as follows:

'Standing, from left: Fr George O'Neill, S.J., fellow of the Royal University, who would become professor of English at U.C.D. after the establishment of the National University and later a famous preacher in Australia; James Joyce, destined to be "the only author in the English language more written about than Shakespeare"; John Marcus O'Sullivan, a future professor of history at U.C.D. and minister for education; Bob Kinahan, later an eminent K.C.; Séamus Clandillon, who would be Ireland's first director of broadcasting; Patrick Semple, professor of Latin at U.C.D. from 1909 to 1947.

Seated, centre row, from left: George Clancy, who as mayor of Limerick would be murdered by the Black and Tans; Fr Edmund Hogan, S.J., fellow of the Royal University and a leading authority on the Irish language; Edouard Cadic, later professor of French at U.C.D.; Fr Joseph Darlington, S.J. (Fr Delany's assistant).

Front row, from left: Felix Hackett, future professor of physics at U.C.D. and president of the Royal Dublin Society; Séamus O'Kelly, a Gaelic scholar who became a medical doctor and lecturer in obstetrics in U.C.D.; Michael Lennon, who became well-known both as a district justice and as a critic of James Joyce; and Con Curran, renowned authority on the architecture of Dublin.'

As Fr Delany's assistant, Fr Joseph Darlington, a former Anglican priest, served as prefect of studies as well as professor of English and later as professor of philosophy. This picture, first published in A page of Irish history: story of University College Dublin 1883-1909, *indicates the calibre of Fr Delany's University College.*

It was ironic that a fund associated with one of the more unhappy episodes in his life should have enabled him to build University Church. The Achilli trial had its origins in the restoration of the Catholic hierarchy in England in 1850, which had prompted a widespread and violent anti-Catholic agitation. Among means resorted to for fanning it was the employment by the Evangelical Alliance of the apostate Dominican priest, named Giovanni Giacinto Achilli (1802-70), to declaim in various parts of the country against the Church of Rome. Dr Achilli was a most inappropriate person to complain about the crimes and hypocrisy of adherents to the Catholic faith, as he himself was a notorious profligate. Newman gave a series of lectures in Birmingham on the restoration of the Catholic hierarchy and during the course of one of them referred to the 'moral turpitude of Achilli with much plainness of speech'.

After Newman's lectures were published in September 1851 he was faced with a charge of libelling Achilli. He put in a general plea of not guilty and then a justification consisting of twenty-three counts in which, specifying time, date and circumstance, he charged Achilli with as many damnatory facts as those named in his lectures. At the trial in June 1852 a number of witnesses, brought for the most part from Italy, gave evidence establishing these facts. The jury, however, influenced by a partisan summing up by the judge, gave their verdict against Newman. *The Times* of 26 June 1852 in a leading article described the proceedings as 'indecorous in their nature, unsatisfactory in their result and little calculated to increase the respect of the people for the administration of justice or the estimation by foreign nations of the English name and character'. In 1853, a motion for a new trial having been refused, Newman was fined £100. His expenses connected with the case amounted to over £14,000. However, these were defrayed by public subscription. This fund for Newman's defence was oversubscribed. Hence his ability to spend some of it on University Church.

As early as July 1859 Newman proposed to Patrick Leahy (1806-75), archbishop of Cashel, and one of the trustees of the university who had served as vice-rector from 1854 to 1857, that he and the other trustees should purchase the University Church. Following this and other appeals from Newman, Dr Woodlock asked the episcopal board at its meeting in October 1861 for a decision in the matter. They deferred the decision. This was due to reservations by Archbishop John MacHale (1791-1881) and some of the other trustees. These reservations centred on: (1) uncertainty as to the duration of the lease of the ground on which the church

Achilli trial

Transfer of Ownership of University Church

23

11. Thomas Murphy, president of University College, Dublin, 1972-85. As registrar he facilitated the erection of the Michael Devlin Memorial Church at Belfield in 1969.

was built. Newman had succeeded in acquiring a lease from the Protestant Blue Coat Hospital for only seventeen years beginning in 1857. In the event, some years later, his successor had the lease extended to 999 years; (2) the trustees took exception to Newman's building the church without their authorisation; (3) at that time, 1861-2, the trustees were planning to move the Catholic University to a thirty-two acre site at Clonliffe West, Drumcondra, which would have left University Church a good distance from the university it was intended to serve.

The question of the payment of Newman was not finally resolved to the satisfaction of all concerned until January 1864. By that time less than half the cost of the church, £2,400, had been made over to Newman, the amount for which he had eventually settled. The trustees also arranged the provision in perpetuity of a weekly Mass for all who had contributed to the church building fund, a fact commemorated by a plaque in the sacristy.

University Church, a Chapel of Ease to St Kevin's

From almost the outset the running costs of the church exceeded its income. Newman's successor, Dr Woodlock, became increasingly anxious about this drain on university funds. Accordingly he arranged that on 1 January 1869 University Church was given by the trustees to the parish of St Kevin's, Harrington Street, which been constituted as a parish from that of St Nicholas of Myra, Francis Street, just four years earlier. Thereby, while the university continued to have full access to the church, it

12. Patrick Masterson, president of University College, Dublin, 1985-93. He inaugurated the three-year, post-graduate category known as 'Newman Scholars' in 1988.

was no longer responsible for its financial liabilities. This happy arrangement continued for University College and its successor, University College, Dublin.

From 1964 onwards various faculties of University College, Dublin, were re-sited at Belfield in the southern Dublin suburbs. In 1968-9 Archbishop John Charles McQuaid (1895-1973) had a university church built on the new campus with funds generously donated by an unassuming philanthropist, named Michael Devlin (1895-1979). From 1986 onwards chaplains to University College, Dublin, resided at Roebuck, near Belfield. Thereafter the new church there, the Michael Devlin Memorial Church, dedicated to Our Lady, Seat of Wisdom, became, in effect, the recognised church of the university. In the meantime, in 1974, University Church had become the church for a newly-constituted parish hived off from St Kevin's, Harrington Street. Although no longer the focus for the religious activities of undergraduates, University Church continues to be a popular venue for the marriages of graduates, religious services associated with class re-unions and for special university occasions. It is also a centre for promoting the beatification and eventually the canonisation of John Henry Newman. To this end there is a special Mass and sermon in October each year. But, above all, University Church remains a monument to Newman in Ireland as the Birmingham Oratory is his monument in England.

University Church, Church of the Parish of Our Lady Seat of Wisdom

13. Newman House, 85-86 St Stephen's Green, and side view of porch of University Church

PART 2

FEATURES OF
UNIVERSITY CHURCH

In 1855 Newman bought 87 St Stephen's Green. Although built in 1730, it was in good structural condition. He had University Church built on the garden beside and behind the house. Today access to the church is through a porch erected a few years after the church was completed. Although of small proportions, it more than hints at the lavish quality of the decoration of the church's interior. Romanesque in style, it is constructed of polychromatic brick with short columns and cushion-capitals bearing the symbols of the four evangelists and the figures of six angels. Above the main door, which is bright red, as are the other doors of the church, is a richly coloured arch topped by three small windows and an ornamental metal cross.

Entrance

Designed by John Hungerford Pollen, the porch was provided at his own expense by Fr William H. Anderdon, chaplain to University Church. Above the porch is the curiously suspended belfry and bell, also later additions to the church. The original bell from this belfry is now in the Administration Block of University College at Belfield, thus linking the new campus with its roots.

Inside the porch is an atrium which one enters by descending six steps. From this, which is, in effect, a passage way between 86 and 87 St Stephen's Green to the church, there is access to the large gallery where Newman envisaged the students of the university would be accommodated. In the atrium there are a number of plaques, including one to Eugene O'Curry which states that he was 'First Professor of Archaeology in this Catholic University' and that 'he died on 30 July 1862 in the 68th year of his age'.

Overall appearance

The church is 120 feet in length, 36 feet in width and 40 feet in height. Its floor is paved with unglazed Staffordshire black and red tiles. The sacristy is behind the sanctuary. On the left is a small Lady chapel which was added in 1875.

The atrium leads into a kind of ante-church, an effect generated by the gallery overhead which extends a further 25 feet into the church. The gallery is supported by arches, beams and marble columns, and other slender pillars. The marble columns have alabaster capitals composed of carved foliage, fruit, flowers and birds. Iron railings, dividing the ante-church from the rest of the church, were added later. In 1990 these were removed and placed in front of small shrines on either side of the church. Here also are the traditional-style stations of the cross.

The church has a flat, red-timbered ceiling, divided into mullioned compartments on which Pollen painted sprays of vines. On the side walls under the roof are the narrow, round-headed windows, grouped irregularly. They are glazed with 'bulls' eyes'. These knots of glass, which form the centre of large sheets and are usually cut away and re-melted, were acquired from a Dublin bottle factory. Financial stringency necessitated the use of this glass and the provision of some of the church's other features, notably some of the pillars under the gallery.

The sanctuary is raised above the level of the nave and is approached by five steps. An alabaster communion rail runs across the centre of the nave leaving access at either end. The alabaster altar frontal has twelve discs of Derbyshire fluorspar crystals. These are set in an alabaster framework in two groups of six. In the centre of the frontal there is an outline of a Byzantine cross. Each of the nine compartments formed by the cross has an inset panel painted on a gold ground. Christ in glory appears on the panel in the centre of the cross; the evangelists, John and Mark, to his right and left Matthew and Luke above and below him. In the corners are the doctors of the Latin Church, Augustine and Ambrose at the top, Gregory and Jerome below.

Pollen recalled that the altar crucifix was executed from his design 'by a clever Dublin tinker'. Three tall candlesticks stand on the altar on either side of the crucifix, their Byzantine shape in keeping with the rest of the decoration. Made of wood they are gilded to took like metal. They were carved to Pollen's design by carpenters employed by the contractor, J. P. Beardwood & Son of Westland Row. The *baldachino* is made of deal and framed into the wall behind. Its five small domes and other decorative carving also give it a Byzantine appearance. Behind the *baldachino,* along the entire width of the apse, runs a broad decorative band with a formal pattern of circles filled with a stylised flower motif, linked by elements of lattice work. The circles and lattice elements are in glazed white ceramic tiles which stand out sharply against the dark red ground, the whole band being enclosed in bright green borders. This band marks the transition from the painted area of the semi-dome to the marble inlay on the lower walls of the apse. It also carries the circle motif from the semi-dome to the area immediately behind the altar which acts as a reredos. Here circular studs of glass are set into a framework of albaster and marble giving a jewelled effect as they reflect the light of the candles on the altar.

14. Interior of University Church 1994

15. The apse, the sanctuary and the altar

The semi-dome above the sanctuary, which was inspired by the apse of San Clemente in Rome, is the glory of University Church. In the centre is the Virgin, enthroned as *Sedes Sapientiae,* Seat of Wisdom. Above her, wings outstretched, is a dove, representing the Holy Spirit, and further up a jewelled cross, representing Christ. At the top rays in brilliant colours emanate from the hand of God. Rising from the centre of the base a vine sends its branches coiling outward in a series of circles which fill the whole space of the semi-dome. In each of the circles, on a dark ground contrasted with the gold, stand virgins of both sexes bearing palm branches. Various kinds of birds, including a pelican, and insects inhabit the tendrils of the vine, and animals, such as deer and rabbits, can be seen among the grass and flowers at its root. These insects and animals are intended to represent the homage of that portion of creation into which sin had not entered or which had been redeemed from it.

A broad border runs along the base of the semi-dome, with a motif of vine branches enclosing small medallions in which there are more birds, on a dark blue ground. Around the inside rim is another border, with the vine branch, laden with grapes against a purple background.

While stressing the similarity between the apse mosaic of San Clemente in Rome and that of University church, art historian, Eileen Kane, has indicated that some of the details in Pollen's apse are derived from other sources. Thus she writes: 'The deer drinking at the fountain is a motif frequently found in Italian mosaics, and the jewelled cross suggests the magnificent Byzantine cross in the apse of Sant' Apollinare in Classe at Ravenna. But there are other memories too in Pollen's apse. The figure of the *Sedes Sapientiae* is Flemish, not Italian, in inspiration and strikingly recalls a wood-carved Virgin enthroned in the Musé des Beaux-Arts at Ghent, which Pollen may have known. On two occasions, at least, before he came to Dublin, John Pollen was in Ghent. He spent long hours in the cathedral there, meditating on the Van Eyck masterpiece "The Adoration of the Lamb" ... Of Von Eyck's work he had written: "The picture is brimful of ideas. His great wish is to represent creation as restored: everything as if the Fall had not been ... Paradise is once again a garden. Its fields studded with violets and white flowers, types of penitence and chastity ..." The palm-bearing saints which fill the medallions in the Dublin apse breathe a certain fragrance of Ghent.'

Newman was delighted with Pollen's artistic work. On 9 November 1856 he wrote to him: '... I write before High Mass. The apse is magnificent ...' And he added a postscript: 'I have come from High Mass. The more I looked at the apse, the more

16. Choir-gallery

The choir-gallery

beautiful it seemed to me – and to my taste, the church is the most beautiful one in the Kingdom.'

The choir-gallery stands on the gospel side of the sanctuary. Access to it is from the sacristy. It is supported by seven marble pillars, each of whose alabaster capitals carry a design based on a plant. The capital nearest the altar has grapes and ears of wheat representing the Blessed Sacrament. Others have passion-flowers, shamrocks, roses, acorns or oak leaves. A gilded wooden screen of pierced lattice panels in varied patterns tops the choir gallery. Newman hoped that the church might one day be served by a community of Oratorians and that they could pray there before the Blessed Sacrament without being observed from the body of the church. Thirty feet long, the choir-gallery is only six feet wide with little space for an organ and probably because of this it was replaced by one constructed in the gallery at the rear of the church soon after Newman returned to England. This was somewhat ironic, as a letter, dated 23 June 1855, to F. S. Bowles, indicates that the first item he thought of providing for the church was an organ: 'Will you tell me what sort of an organ you would recommend me to get, as to stops etc., for £250? I have signed an agree-

ment for the ground this day – and shall begin building my church at once. I have already been with the organ builder, Telford, who is a good man.'

The pulpit

Opposite the choir-gallery and outside the sanctuary is the pulpit supported on four pillars of polished marble, bearing the symbols and names of the four evangelists. It is approached by a stone staircase with an alabaster balustrade and is encased with panels of marble of various colours. Its imposing size indicates the emphasis placed by Newman on preaching. It seems he hoped to make Dublin, as he had made Oxford, a centre of religion as well as learning and to exercise an influence in his new surroundings as he had in the pulpit of St Mary's University Church in Oxford twenty years earlier. Newman also intended to use sermons as a means of 'interesting the clergy in the university, the preachers being taken from all parts of the country', and many distinguished preachers declaimed here particularly during the decade after the church was built. In the present century most well-known preachers from the English-speaking world have graced this pulpit, generally on the occasion of the annual retreat for the students of University College. The pulpit is covered by a canopy on two marble pillars, between which is a beautiful ivory and ebony crucifix with Mary and St John represented at the foot of the cross.

The lateral walls The lateral walls are lavishly decorated with three bands of marbles of different shapes and colours to a height of fifteen feet. There is black marble from Kilkenny, green from Galway, red from Cork and brown and grey from Armagh and Offaly. In the first band the alabaster capitals of the fictive pillars between these marble slabs depict the life cycle of birds. In the second band are eleven large arch-shaped panels. These contain lunettes painted by Pollen. Three are on the sanctuary wall opposite the choir-gallery and there are four on each side of the nave. Each lunette has, in the centre, a standing saint with an angel on either side. Decorative foliage fills the lower corners. All the paintings have a gold-coloured background.

The saints depicted were chosen for their appropiateness to the church built as a university church in Dublin at that time. On the right, looking towards the altar, in the sanctuary lunettes are two of the patrons of Ireland, St Patrick and St Brigid, and the patron of Dublin, St Laurence O'Toole. On the right wall above the pulpit is St Peter. Below the pulpit the series continues with St Paul. Then comes St Dominic, St Anthony of Padua, St Philip Neri and Blessed John de Britto. On the left wall facing the last four are St Benedict, St Thomas Aquinas, St Fiachre and St Ignatius Loyola. St Dominic and St Benedict are represented because both were founders of religious orders with a long tradition of scholarship. St Thomas Aquinas and St Anthony of Padua were both university lecturers, the one taught in the University of Paris, the other in the University of Bologna. St Philip Neri was the founder of the Oratorians which Newman had joined after his ordination in Rome. St Fiachre spent his life evangelising in the Loire valley in France and represented Ireland's missionary activity in Europe and beyond. St Ignatius Loyola had founded the Society of Jesus and Blessed John de Britto, one of his spiritual sons martyred in India, had recently been beatified.

Above the third band of marbles and a gilt moulding, the upper lateral walls carry a series of large paintings which are now so darkened as to be almost indecipherable. Attempts in 1962, 1979 and 1991 to correct this darkening of the pictures by having them cleaned were ineffectual. The darkening process, it seems, is in part due to the still-wet plaster when they were put up and the porous canvas on which the pictures were painted. The result is that they can only be seen now in bright early morning light. The models for these pictures were tapestries which Raphael designed for the Sistine Chapel and the figures of the apostles from the abbey

18. Section of lateral walls, including Sir Thomas Farrell's bust of Newman

church of Tre Fontaine outside Rome. The pictures, which were painted in Rome, are the work of MM. Sublet and Souslacroix of Lyons. Looking towards the altar and moving back from it, on the left wall are: 'The stoning of St Stephen', 'St. Paul at Lystra', 'The blinding of Elymas' and 'The healing of the lame man at the beautiful gate'. On the right wall moving towards the altar are the 'Death of Ananias', 'The miraculous draught of fishes', 'Christ's threefold commission to St Peter', 'St Paul preaching at Athens', 'The conversion of St Paul' and 'The descent of the Holy Spirit'. Between these cartoons, paintings of the twelve apostles are interspersed.

19. Lady chapel   The Lady chapel was built in 1875 as a gift from Justice William O'Brien (1832-99) who later, in 1899, was the first benefactor of the library of the Milltown Institute of Theology and Philosophy. Entry to the Lady chapel is by two steps under the choir-gallery. The windows in this side chapel depict 'The nativity', 'The adoration of the wise men' and 'Christ with the doctors in the temple'. The Marian statue is that of 'Our Lady, assumed into heaven'. The baptismal font, where an extraordinary cross-section of Irish persons, both the famous and the not so famous, have begun their lives as Christians, stands in the chapel.

A bust of Newman completed by Sir Thomas Farrell (1827-1900) in 1892 occupies a niche half way up the church on the right hand side. The inscription reads: **Other features**

John Henry Cardinal Newman
Born 1801. Died 1890
Rector of the Catholic University of Ireland 1854-1859
R.I.P.

Nearby is a medallion portrait of Thomas Arnold, brother of Matthew, the poet, with the inscription:

In tender memory of
Thomas Arnold M.A. Second Son of
Dr Arnold of Rugby. B. Nov. 30, 1823
d. Nov. 12, 1900. Educated at Winchester,
Rugby and Oxford. Fellow of The
Royal University of Ireland &
Professor of English Language
& Literature in
University College, Dublin.

Domine Deus Meus In Te Speravi.

Life of John Henry Newman
in *haiku*[1]

MADELEINE KISNER

Scholar, vicar, priest,
the subject of these tercets,
John Henry Newman.

Born in London town
Twenty-one February
Eighteen-hundred-one!

His father was John
And his mother Jemima.
The children were six.

At the Ealing School
Newman met Walter Mayers
Who influenced him.

Eighteen-seventeen
John was at Trinity
But failed his exams.

Then to Oriel.
A fellowship he received.
And was eminent.

Newman's father died.
Then John was a deacon in
The Anglican Church.

A college tutor
Newman became for four years
and then a vicar.

---

1. The *haiku* is a Japanese poetic form of three lines with seventeen syallables, five in the first and third lines and seven in the second. Ordinarily *haiku* focuses on an image in nature; here it encapsulates events in Newman's life.

Saint Mary's, Oxford,
And the parish, Littlemore,
Received his sermons.

On a tour abroad
In Sicily illness struck.
Wrote 'Lead Kindly Light'.

Back to Oxford then,
Newman heard Keble's sermon,
Oxford movement born!

The Church of England
Must be reformed and return
To Catholic roots.

The leaders were three:
Newman, Keble and Pusey.
A crusade began!

Eighteen thirty-six
Newman's grief renewed once more
When his mother died.

He wished to adapt
The thirty-nine articles
With R.C. doctrine.

Tract number Ninety
Dealt Newman a heavy blow –
Condemned by the Heads.

Via Media
Newman could not ever find.
The Truth must be faced.

Founded on study
Of the early Church Fathers
Newman's life was changed.

'The parting of friends'
Was Newman's farewell sermon
That brought tears to eyes.

Confident in God
He followed the Kindly Light
And left Oriel.

On October ninth
John was brought into the Fold,
Eighteen-forty-five.

A Passionist priest,
Named Dominic Barberi,
Baptised him that night.

Off to Rome he went
With Ambrose St John his friend.
John was now a priest.

Then to Birmingham
To found the Congregation
Of Philip Neri.

This Oratory,
Proposed for secular priests,
Became John's haven.

Newman's pen poured forth,
Loss and Gain and *Callista*,
As his two novels.

Loss and Gain gave some
Autobiographical
Accounts of John's life.

Callista was set
In the persecution times
Of the Holy Church.

Newman gave lectures.
Wrote articles 'To consult
The faithful in doctrine'.

Papal decrees brought
New Catholic hierarchy
To appointed sees.

Cardinal Wiseman
Appointed to Westminster.
John saw bright future.

The Achilli case
Aided the undermining
Of the Catholics.

Achilli met John
When he was in Birmingham.
Newman exposed him.

Newman took advice
From Wiseman's written account.
Achilli brought suit.

Newman lost the case –
Two years of legal delays.
But God was with him.

John was then rector
Of Dublin's Catholic U.,
An arduous task.

A new church he held
Would give spiritual aid
To the students there.

John Newman summoned
A John Hungerford Pollen
As his architect.

The Byzantine style
From basilicas in Rome
Appealed to both men.

On Saint Stephen's Green,
In Dublin, is Newman's church,
Next to Newman House.

There is Farrell's work,
A marble bust of Newman,
Two memorials!

In spite of problems
The University grew
And made some progress.

In his 'Discourses',
Classic in Education,
John starts his great work.

The Idea aimed
At a unified knowledge,
Known as 'Liberal'.

This knowledge he held
Led to a habit of mind
That would last always.

Freedom and calmness
Moderation and wisdom –
Would be qualities.

Newman's *Idea*
Held theology a branch
Of knowledge also.

Newman's 'Discourses'
And his series of lectures
Were *The Idea.*

Newman left Ireland
With warm and friendly feelings,
In spite of troubles.

John was editor
Of the Catholic journal,
Known as *The Rambler.*

Writing treatise
'On consulting the faithful',
He was soon denounced.

Newman had to learn
God's will acts in many ways
Even years later.

The Oratory
In eighteen-sixty and two
Had problems galore.

Newman had a task
To reappoint his whole staff.
It was near collapse.

A written attack
In a Charles Kingsley review
Greatly perturbed John.

How could he reply?
Apologia he wrote
To rebut the charge.

Apologia
Was a notable success.
John was justified.

But there were concerns
Both with Ward and with
Manning, now a cardinal.

Newman and Manning
Had many difficulties.
Letters told the rift.

Eighteen-seventy
And Vatican Council One
Sealed *Ex Cathedra.*

By seventy-five
A controversy arose
With Gladstone's defeat.

Papal extremists
Distorted Gladstone's vision
About one's conscience.

Newman's 'A letter
To His Grace, Duke of Norfolk'
Was in pamphlet form.

The duke was John's friend,
Victim of Gladstone's attack,
In Newman's 'letter'.

'A letter' received –
Both men were considerate.
Gladstone thanked Newman.

Trials began once more.
Newman's friend Ambrose St John
Soon fell ill and died.

Newman's grief was great.
No one could know his sad loss.
They share the same grave.

Oxford's Trinity
Issued John invitation
As honor. fellow.

Newman felt quite pleased
That his College remembered.
Did Oriel forget?

What a great honour –
Oxford still banned Catholics,
Yet Newman could come.

As time took its toll –
Pope Pius the Ninth had died.
Leo made pontiff.

Pope Leo Thirteenth,
Adding lustre to the Church,
Acclaimed John Newman.

Eighteen-sev'nty-nine
Newman was made cardinal
By Leo Thirteenth.

Newman begged to die
Where he lived at Birmingham
Rather than at Rome.

But John travelled there
For audience with the pope.
Leo was gracious.

Despite failing health,
Newman kept on his preaching
And sat for portraits!

In eighteen-ninety,
On eleventh of August,
Newman passed away.

Buried at Rednal,
In the grave of his dear friend,
Newman lies at rest.

The stone as inscribed
with 'From shadows and image
Into truth' says all.

Newman, we hail you,
As man, as educator,
In your search for truth.

We pray your sainthood
Will give us courage and strength
To follow the 'Light'.

Lead, Kindly Light[1]

Lead, Kindly Light, amid the encircling gloom.
Lead Thou me on!
The night is dark, and I am far from home.
Lead Thou me on!
Keep Thou my feet: I do not ask to see
The distant scene – one step enough for me.

I was not ever thus, nor pray'd that Thou
Shouldst lead me on.
I loved to choose and see my path, but now
Lead Thou me on!
I loved the garish day, and, in spite of fears,
Pride ruled my will: remember not past years.

So long Thy power hath blest me, sure it still
Will lead me on.
O'er moor and fen, o'er crag and torrent, till
The night is gone;
And with the morn those angel faces smile
Which I have loved long since, and lost awhile.

1. In his *Apologia Pro Vita Sua* (Oxford 1864) Newman, having recalled that during a visit to Italy he had become gravely ill in Sicily, described the circumstances in which he composed this prayer as follows: 'I was aching to get home; yet for want of a vessel I was kept at Palermo for three weeks ... At last I got off in an orange boat bound for Marseilles. Then it was that I wrote the lines "Lead, Kindly Light" which have since become well-known. We were becalmed a whole week in the Straits of Bonifacio.'

John Hungerford Pollen's account of the building of University Church[1]

I am now going to ask your indulgence, before finishing this course of lectures, for going into some account of a more humble attempt to erect a basilica, with poor resources and small command of skill, for the use of our own university.

Why, independently of artistic reasons, was the basilica form chosen? ...

... The basilicas exhibit a system of internal architecture; now this decoration is less costly, and far easier, than that of exteriors; and, if the one only can be effected, more consonant to the Christian spirit; for there was this striking point of contrast between temples of the old worship and the houses of the new; here the worshippers themselves entered, and heard and saw the mysteries within ... I have no wish to undervalue Gothic, the loftiest production of design in the modern world; but Gothic in its true home is mostly external in its beauty. To be sublime in the old manner, it needs to be dramatic, and costly beyond calculation – witness Cologne – and to make Gothic grand with small means is a problem which I do not think modern architects have solved; at least but rarely.

Preaching, again, was a primary object in the scope of the design; and, therefore, on all acoustic principles, it was desirable that the inside of the building should be as little broken up as possible.

Naturally, too, in an institution like ours, yet in a state of infancy, and designed to draw out and deepen the heart and intelligence of the nation, we wished to set the example of developing, as far as our resources went, the natural capabilities of Ireland; and, geologically, the most valuable of these are the various veins of marble so plentifully compacted under and over the soil, on every coast and in every county ... All these requirements, and more, were better to be fulfilled in a basilica than in any other kind of building. In order to avail ourselves to the utmost, to the very utmost of our small space, I had the foundations laid in part below our boundary wall, so as both to strengthen that, and also to enable us to build up against it.

1. This is taken from lecture vi of 'Lectures on the Basilicas' delivered in the Catholic University, Dublin, in 1855 by John Hungerford Pollen, professor of fine arts.

The ground plan is a parallelogram, 100 feet with 20 added, and an apse of 25 feet diameter or 12.6 radius; a total of 132 feet by 35 of general width. The cubic height is 40 feet; the pitch of the roof no higher than is necessary for protection from weather. Thus our general design is as simple as a building can possibly be. The additional 20 feet opens by two colonnades of elliptical arches into the principal nave. In order to obtain as much strength as possible, and as dry a wall as could be got in so damp a climate, the church itself, all except the additional 20 feet, is of brick.

The light is obtained by rows of narrow arched windows on either side. The reasons for placing all the apertures to the main building on one level, and as high as possible, will be obvious to anyone who observes the effect of having all the light descending, so as to give the whole of the wall decorations the best possible chance of showing themselves, and to avoid in any way breaking on the serious serenity of the lower space, by dazzling openings and correlative contrasts of shade. I was amused, whilst the building was in progress, at the almost universal complaint of my friends, unused to this method of lighting, that we should be in positive darkness. Of course the dark irreflective colour of the raw brick-work, and the quantity of scaffolding, deceived them; the fact being that the greatest possible amount of light transmissible by windows is obtained by their being placed as high as they can be. The same quantity of glazed openings two-thirds down the wall would have left us in the dark, near as they might be to the eye. The only decoration I attempted to these windows, in which the glass was necessarily white, was to obtain from the English glass works a sufficient number of 'bulls eyes' or knots of glass forming the centre of large sheets (and usually cut away and re-melted) to glaze the whole. I do not know how many thousands are used. It will be observed that every window without exception is thus glazed, in order not to break their absolute uniformity by calling attention to features which have no claim to observation. A certain brilliancy, play of delicate colour, and, if I may so call it, quiet confusion, is obtained; but nothing more.

For these buildings, I myself prefer the open roof structure; but this, for acoustic reasons, was impossible. I therefore had the joists and beams laid out, and laid my flat ceiling above them. The space was thus reticulated over with a very quiet and uniform subdivision; the frame, such as it is, I left in the rough, not wishing to spend any money on it, even for fine coats of plaster. On the mortar I painted, in tempera, a foliated design in one colour, so as still to preserve the flat unpretending character of a feature somewhat poor. The timbers I painted red and decorated with white designs, flat also, that colour giving the utmost size and dignity to such slight work.

The floor was the commonest and cheapest procurable, consistent with durability. It was of coarse unglazed Staffordshire tile, in two colours, red and black, and of one size. These, however, instead of the usual house pattern of alternative squares and diamonds, I laid in designs, the general plan embracing the entire area of the building.

To provide for the choir of singers without encroaching on the space appropriated to the public, we adopted a basilican gallery, 30 feet long, with commodious width: 6 feet. Its position would offend the shallow notions of those critics who must needs see everything on one side of a building balanced by a 'ditto' opposite, but it was so dignified in itself that we had no hesitation in placing it where it would be most useful – as near both altar and sanctuary as convenient. All necessary arrangements have a meaning: and, unless very unartistically managed, explain the uses of a building, and are a source of interest.

Both galleries are supported on elliptical arches, resting on monolithic columns of the different Irish marbles.

*   *   *

After these constructive parts came the more serious and difficult question of the decoration. The side walls are all crusted over with marbles in the peculiar mode called by the ancients *opus musivum*; no raised panellings as in the Gothic or modern Italian methods, only flat *intarsiature* without relief.

*   *   *

This inlaid marble is bordered and incorporated into the wall by a string or running mould in the Byzantine manner, of Caen stone, roughed over with flat lines and covered with gold. The end wall in which the apse opens forms the representative of the old triumphal arch.

*   *   *

The altar was necessarily pushed back into the apse; nor for lack of space could our *baldacchino* be supported on columns. It is framed roof-wise into the wall behind, and carried down on brackets. The *baldacchino* is of common deal, and is intended to be gilded and decorated.

*   *   *

The divisions of the altar design are obvious; the twelve typical precious stones each side of the central Byzantine cross, with a Christ in glory and the four evangelists and four doctors radiating round Him. I introduced, something after the old Byzantine manner, pierced lattice in place of curtains in the singers' gallery, and pierced work in the *baldacchino* of the altar and pulpit. One of the joiners employed in the building carried this out to my complete satisfaction. The altar crucifix was executed from a design of my own by a clever Dublin tinker. The candlesticks we could not afford in metal; I had them carved – first myself drawing the entire design on each mass of wood – by the men employed on the spot.

The golden apse, and the side arched panels with a rude mosaic round them, ought to tell their own story. The apse is divided by a mystic vine into circular frames, each containing saints; virgins of either sex surrounding the *Sedes Sapientiae* in the centre, as types of immaculate purity. The field below and the branches have birds, insects and animals, intended to represent the homage of that portion of creation into which sin has not entered, or which has been redeemed from it. The outer wall of the triumphal arch is to contain (some day or other) designs of the prophets and apostles.

*   *   *

We have decorations still to place on many parts of our wall surface, the altar to complete, the divers details for which there are as yet no funds; and we propose a portico opening on St Stephen's Green, to give entrance to the vestibule, as soon as the same unpleasant reason ceases to extinguish our powers.

A thousand other details of difficulties, and of resources to meet them, natural to an undertaking new to most of us, I might yet relate; but I must now have exhausted your patience, and will only point out once again what resources there are in Ireland, and in the intelligence and quickness of her ordinary workmen, whose patience and docility, in a number of operations altogether strange to them, enabled me to carry out much that could ordinarily be entrusted only to craftsmen of long training. There is, too, this advantage to an architect; that he gets in such circumstances men who have little to unlearn. What we want in our building is a prevailing idea; spirited work, calculated to produce its effects at the proper distance. Professed carvers would have attempted smoothness and what they call finish, and so ruined the design. The degrading softness and effeminacy of so much of our most careful modern work is the bane of architects, as, I am sure, all thoughtful men of that profession would allow.[2]

2. How did John Pollen achieve his artistic success? In the closing words of the last of six 'Lectures on woodcarving' delivered at South Kensington, *c.* 1878, he thus speaks for himself: 'Life is short, art is long. Long, because it asks from us so long a study. Art is a translation of some aspects of that lovely creation in which we live. Art translates into a language and writes with letters of its own. It takes long to learn this language; long to fashion the hand to write these characters with grace and skill … Art is long; perfection is unattainable. Unattainable, according to the ideal of the artist; yet, in a measure, perfection has from time to time been reached; and that in an astonishing manner. What has been the secret of this occasional success? The answer is simple indeed; it has been by love, by courage, by modesty, by patient but determined perseverance.'

51

SOURCES

A
UNPUBLISHED WORK

Dublin, The Irish Architectural Archive, 73 Merrion Square, Structural Report (University Church, St Stephen's Green) by Stanislaus Kenny and Partners 1969.

Dublin, Fr Liam Rigney, Presbytery, North William Street, 'Bartholomew Woodlock and the Catholic University of Ireland 1861-79' (Ph.D. thesis, University College, Dublin 1995).

B
PUBLISHED WORKS

A page of Irish history: story of University College Dublin 1883-1909 (compiled by Fathers of the Society of Jesus) (Dublin 1930).

'Architectural description of the University Church', *Catholic University Gazette,* April 1856.

Blackrock College Annual 1978.

Corish, P. J., *Maynooth College 1795-1995* (Dublin 1995).

Costello, Peter, *Dublin churches* (Dublin 1989).

Curran C. P., *Newman House and University Church* (Dublin, n.d.).

Dessain, C. S. and others (eds.), *The letters and diaries of John Henry Newman* (London 1961-).

Elrington Ball, F., *The judges in Ireland 1221-1921* (London 1926).

Fitzpatrick, S. A. O., *Dublin, a historical and topographical account of the city* (Dublin 1907).

Flood, J. M., 'A link with Newman', *New Ireland* 4,11 September 1915.

Kane, Eileen, 'John Henry Newman's Catholic University Church in Dublin', *Studies,* summer/autumn 1977.

Letters and notices, vol. 20 (1889-90) (Roehampton 1889-90).

McGrath, S.J., Fergal, *Newman's University: idea and reality* (London 1951).

McRedmond, Louis, *Thrown among strangers: John Henry Newman in Ireland* (Dublin 1990).

—, *To the greater glory: a history of the Irish Jesuits* (Dublin 1991).

Martin, Gerry, 'The "Quasi-rebels" ', *The bulletin of the Society of St Vincent de Paul in Ireland,* autumn 1996.

Meenan, P. N., 'The Medical School: the first phase', *U.C.D. News,* November 1980.

Morrissey, S.J., T. J., *Towards a National University: William Delany, S.J. (1835-1924)* (Dublin 1983).

Neville, W. P. (ed.), *My campaign in Ireland Part 1: Catholic University reports and other papers by Cardinal Newman of the Oratory* (Aberdeen 1896).

Newman, J. H., *Apologia Pro Vita Sua: being a history of his religious opinions* (London 1890).

O'Brien, Jacqueline, and Guinness, Desmond, *Dublin: a grand tour* (London 1994).

O'Loughlin, Thomas, *Cardinal Newman: seeker of truth* (Dublin 1988).

O'Reilly, Seán, and Rowan, Alistair, *University College Dublin* (Dublin 1990).

Pollen, Anne, *John Hungerford Pollen 1820-1902* (London 1912).

Sherry, Richard, *Holy Cross College, Clonliffe, Dublin* (Dublin 1962).

White, Norman, *Hopkins: a literary biography* (Oxford 1992).

Wilson, R. F., *Newman's church in Dublin* (Dublin 1916).

C
PERSONS

Comerford, Seán, University Church, St Stephen's Green, Dublin 2.

Heffernan, Fr Brendan, St Anne's, Strand Road, Portmarnock, Co Dublin.

McCartney, Professor Donal, 30 Thorncliffe Park, Dublin 14.

Rigney, Fr Liam, Presbytery, North William Street, Dublin 1.

Sheehy, David A., Diocesan Archives, Archbishop's House, Dublin 9.

INDEX

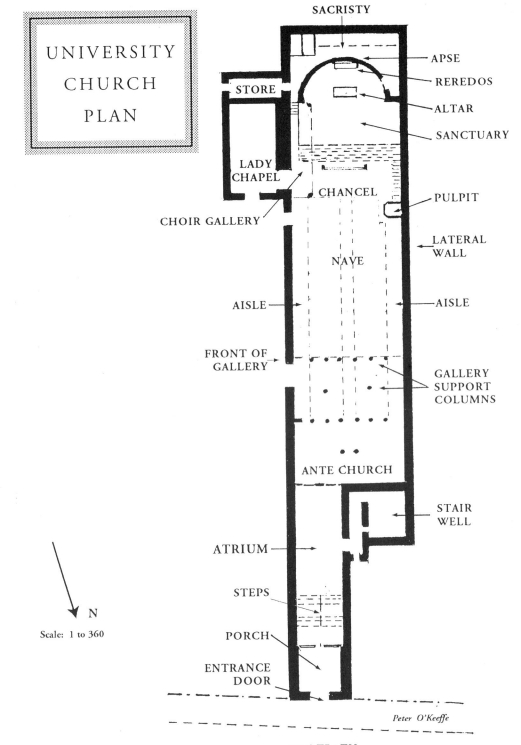

SACRISTY

APSE

REREDOS

STORE

ALTAR

SANCTUARY

UNIVERSITY
CHURCH
PLAN

LADY
CHAPEL

CHANCEL

PULPIT

CHOIR GALLERY

LATERAL
WALL

NAVE

AISLE

AISLE

FRONT OF
GALLERY

GALLERY
SUPPORT
COLUMNS

ANTE CHURCH

STAIR
WELL

ATRIUM

N

STEPS

Scale: 1 to 360

PORCH

ENTRANCE
DOOR

Peter O'Keeffe

20. Plan of church

FOOTPATH
ST STEPHENS GREEN, SOUTH

BIBL. COLLEGII
S.S. CORDIS
S.J. LIMERICK